Estella
A True Story

By Estella V. Shivers

Edited by Mark H. Newhouse

Illustrated by Daniel Traynor

Estella: A True Story
By Estella Shivers

Cover and Illustrations by Daniel Traynor
Edited by Mark H. Newhouse

AimHi Press
Orlando, Florida
www.AimHiPress.com
© 2018, Estella Shivers

Library of Congress Control Number: 2018958044
ISBN: 978-1-945493-10-2 (Paperback)

Names: Shiver, Estella. | Traynor, Daniel, illustrator. | Newhouse, Mark, Editor.
Title: Estella: A True Story / by Estella Shivers
Description: Orlando, FL :AimHi Press, 2018. | Summary: What secret did Estella learn about her mother that changed her life? In this beautifully illustrated, heart-warming, true story, follow Estella, a girl living in a poor village in Nicaragua, as she learns what growing up really means.
Identifiers: LCCN 2018958044 (print) | ISBN 978-1-945493-10-2 (paperback)

Subjects: CYAC: Autobiography. | Mulitcultural. |Latin America. | Family Values. | Coming of age.
Classification: LCC PZ7.1.S55 Es 2018 (print)
LC record available at https://lccn.loc.gov/2018958044

All rights reserved. No part of the material protected by this copyright may be reproduced or utilized in any form by any means without permission in writing from the copyright owner.

*This book is dedicated to
the children in my loving family:*

Devonté Nasir,
Jadalyn Alexus,
JaLia Amina,
Jon'elle Elizabeth,
Eryka GloriRose,
Lamar Alexander

We lived in a small village in Nicaragua. We were very poor.
Mother did not have a good education.

To give us food, Mama washed and ironed clothes for richer families.

Mama took pride in her work, so her customers liked her, and she had much work to do.

It was very hot, so I slept with an open window.
I was often awakened by the birds and chickens, nature's orchestra.

But one morning I heard a different sound.
It was louder than the sounds of the barnyard animals.

The air was filled with the smell of dirty laundry and soap. Rubbing sleep from my eyes, I saw Mama's arms moving quickly up and down the wash board.

Sweat fell from Mama's face, but she kept on working.
I felt like crying.

I was tired, but dressed quickly while my sister slept.

Although exhausted, Mama tied a clothes line from one tree to another.

She hammered a tall stick into the hard earth to keep the middle of the line high, so the clothes would not hit the ground.

"Mama, I'm here to help."
I reached for the bag of clothes pins.

Mama smiled.
"O.K. darling, I'm glad you're here."

Mama picked up a dress and reached down to my hands for the pins.

I kept handing Mama clothespins,
and she kept hanging-up clothes,
until the entire wash was finally done

Boy, did I feel happy when Mama looked at me and smiled. There was nothing she needed to say.

Unfortunately, it began to drizzle.

A strong wind whipped the clothes back and forth, as if they were dancing to the whistling sound of the coming storm.

Mama shouted, "Estella, come quickly.
We need to take down the clothes before the rain!"
I ran to her as fast as I could.

"Is the bag ready for the clothes pins?"
Mama shouted in the wind and rain.

"Yes Mama, it's right here.
Remember, we are a team."

We placed all the clothes in a big tub.

We finished just in time. A huge burst of rain and wind began. We ran as fast as we could.

Once again, that smile from my mother appeared.
I thought we were finished with our work, but . . .

I followed my mother to the kitchen where she pulled out a large sack of flour.

"What are you doing now, Mama?" I asked,
seeing how tired she looked.
"I have to make the starch," she replied.

"Mama, can I help you?"
She nodded, with her usual soft smile.

Making the starch was fun. Flour flew into the air, my face, the floor, and all over my clothes.

Mama laughed and then added water to the flour to make starch.

"This is fun, Mama.
Can I help you again?"

"You can help me as many times as you want, once you learn how to keep the flour in the pan and not all over me." mother laughed.

The next morning, I was awakened by the usual melody
of the chickens and birds,
but there was another sound and a familiar smell.

I followed the smell to the kitchen.

The smell was starch. Mama was ironing the clothes. She sprinkled the starch we made on a shirt.

There was no electricity in our village,
so Mama had to use a very heavy hot iron.

She tested it on a scrap of cloth.
"We can't afford to burn the rich family's clothing," she said.

I never knew how hard Mama worked.
"Good morning Mama. Do you need help?"

I helped by handing her clothing
and then folding them after they were ironed.

When we were finally finished,
it was almost dark.

Mama let me come with her
to deliver the laundry.

The happy customers handed her a few coins, just enough to last us until the next job.

By the time we got home,
the stars were out.

I was never so tired. Mama smiled at me and said, "Estella, now you are a big girl."

I felt proud.

My life in Nicaragua wasn't easy, but I learned valuable lessons that day, ones that would last me all my life.

Estella Victoria Shivers, *was born in a poor village of Nicaragua where her mother worked doing laundry to keep the family fed. At the age of nine, she moved to America where she attended school and became a private secretary.*

Her book, entitled, A Long Journey To The White Picket Fence & Green Grass, *is an autobiography about her early life.*

Today she lives in Florida where she and her husband John are very happy.

Illustrator Daniel Traynor *is a central Florida based artist who has illustrated dozens of children's books. He earned a Bachelor's of Fine Art and Design degree from Eastern Michigan University and worked as a Graphic Designer and Artist for 25 years.*

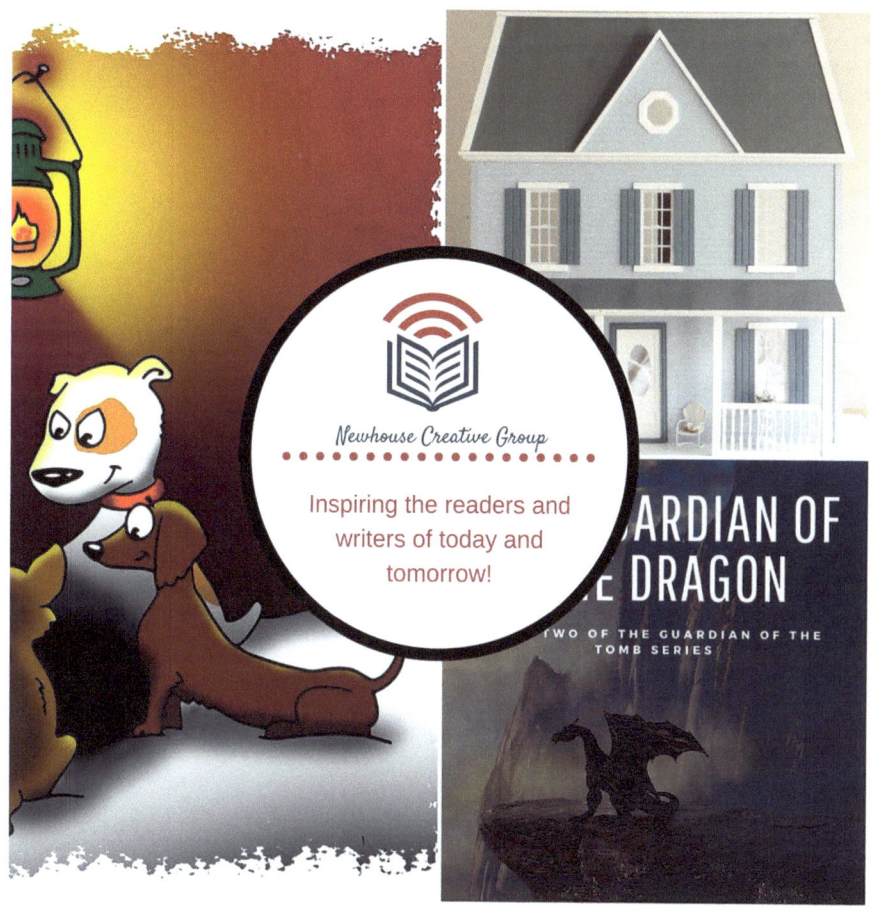

Visit NewhouseCreativeGroup.com for more books
and other products from AimHi Press
and the rest of the Newhouse Creative Group family!

www.ingramcontent.com/pod-product-compliance
Lightning Source LLC
Chambersburg PA
CBHW042122040426
42450CB00002B/43